The Menace

Government

&

Britain's Graveyard

by

A.K. Chesterton

The A.K. Chesterton Trust

2015

This second edition of the combined work is *The A.K. Chesterton Trust Reprint Series* No. 2

Printed & Published in 2015.

ISBN: 978-0-9932885-2-4

© **The A.K. Chesterton Trust, BM Candour, London, WC1N 3XX, United Kingdom.**

Website: www.candour.org.uk

The Menace of World Government and *Britain's Graveyard* were originally published in *Candour*, and went on to be published separately in booklet format in the late 1950's by The League of Empire Loyalists.

This booklet is dedicated to the memory of Dr. Kevan Bleach.

Dr. Kevan Bleach

Foreword

The A.K. Chesterton Trust is proud to publish this booklet - the second in *The A.K. Chesterton Trust Reprint Series*.

The Menace of World Government and *Britain's Graveyard* by A.K. Chesterton have been out of print since the 1950's. Reading these articles once again one cannot help but be impressed by the pin-point accuracy of Arthur Kenneth Chesterton's forecasts. Impressed, but not surprised.

At this very moment we are facing the greatest global financial disaster in history. This is the moment that the New World Order, call it what you will, and their stooges have laid the groundwork for. The supermarkets will be stripped empty in hours and the recent skirmishes in some of the cities and towns in parts of our country will be seen in the correct perspective. The police could not deal with even that very limited disorder. As for stocking up the freezer and pulling the curtains shut? Forget it unless you have a generator with unlimited fuel supplies and the means to protect them. Not forgetting yourself and yours.

There is still a lot of good information out there if you look hard. Stock up on water purification tablets. Packets of vegetable seeds. Buy good quality gardening tools. Put together a first aid kit. The list is endless but if you do not start now....

If you believe I am exaggerating the situation think again. A.K. told us what was coming. His last book was titled *Facing the Abyss* for crying out loud!

A.K. knew how useless and degenerate 'our' people would become in an incredibly short time. Racially alien immigrants and their feral white allies, of all classes it must be noted, are already taking from

Britons all they have. They believe it is their right. They have been told so often that it is.

Do we honestly believe that they have a conscience like you and I?

We have updated the text with footnotes to explain some of the acronyms used and to give some information on the people mentioned.

We would like to thank Jeff Carson for his suggestions, and for proofreading the text.

Colin Todd

The A.K. Chesterton Trust
October 2015

THE MENACE OF WORLD GOVERNMENT

By A. K. Chesterton

The Charter of the United Nations being due for review, considerable pressure is being exerted by various interested bodies to have the United Nations converted into an all-powerful World Government, with sole control of armaments and military forces. Although this would involve a surrender of national sovereignty and independence by Great Britain, more than 100 Members of Parliament are supporting the movement. Such support, in our view, is difficult, if not impossible, to reconcile with their oath "to bear true allegiance to her Sovereign Majesty Queen Elizabeth."

TOWARDS WORLD SLAVERY

World Government involves the surrender to an international police force of all national arms. It is an attractive case to argue before the bulk of electors, in as far as most people are politically superficial, and in as far as their ignorance nowadays is often accompanied by atrophied instincts. That is why it is so dangerous.

The attraction for Britons of the case for World Government is that it conjures up for them the image of a supranational Cabinet consisting of amiable men like themselves, giving orders on the international level to the counterpart of nice, kind London Bobbies who will say to naughty, aggressive nations: "You can't do that 'ere," and by the simple magic of that formula banish forever the possibility of war.

Whose standards?

Everything is made to seem very simple and easy. The invariable assumption is that what will be enforced upon mankind are British standards of civilised conduct and compliance with the British sense of fair play. As the inhabitants of the United Kingdom are outnumbered four to one by the inhabitants of the Soviet Union, and twelve to one, or thereabouts, by the inhabitants of Red China, some allowance should surely be made for the likelihood that the international police would look more like Mongols than Cockneys, and that the standards of decency and fair play which they imposed might well be Russian and Chinese rather than British.

Simple M.P.

A British Member of Parliament, in a recent debate on World Government, indignantly denied that there could be any such development. That development, he said, was not what he had in mind. "I would not stand for it," he declared, thus showing himself to be blissfully unaware of the realities of power as a factor in human affairs. The truth, of course, is that absolute power over H-bomb police would render futile all other power; no constitutional safeguard could prevail against it. History is crammed with instances to show that safeguards and other rights and promises operate only to the extent that the wielders of effective power allow them to operate.

Germany in the First World War laid down her arms upon terms, yet Versailles was a dictated treaty and the victors never honoured their word. Hitler secured the backing of the Ruhr industrialists by promising to introduce anti-labour legislation, but the moment he had consolidated his power he tore up that promise before their eyes. Our own country was in a solemn treaty relationship with the Indian Princes; when the British Government's obligations became inconvenient they were jettisoned. Natal joined the Union of South Africa on the understanding that the Union would remain in perpetuity a British Dominion, but notwithstanding the entrenched clauses in the Constitution she is now in grave danger of becoming part of an Afrikaner republic.

Fatuous Theory

How fatuous, when even nations with honourable traditions so often break their pledged words and sacrifice principle to expediency, to suppose that international power-masters would display a meticulous regard for paper constitutions circumscribing the exercise of their power. Once they had secured control of the H-bomb police, the world would be theirs to command. Yet that is the thesis which members of every established political party in Britain ask the British people to accept. Its proponents do not even begin to meet the objection to their arguments by saying simply that they ask no more than that nations renounce the right to make war. The renunciation of that right would carry with it the implicit renunciation of all other rights, because in the last resort a nation's arms would be its only means of staying out, or contracting out, of what would almost certainly become an international slave state of the Soviet model.

Lurid Light

The Second London Parliamentary Conference on World Government shed a lurid light on the projected internationalist Utopia which it is hoped to foist upon mankind. "Every person in the world," it declared, "should be a citizen of the United Nations as well as of his own country, and the Charter and laws should bind each individual.... The U.N. Police should be strategically placed; it would not be open to a State to refuse the presence of the U.N. Police on its soil.... The Statute of the International Court of Justice should be amended so as to empower it to exercise criminal jurisdiction over any individual accused of offences against international law." Britons can scarcely be expected to enjoy the thought of a midnight knock on the door by a posse of Mongolian or Liberian members of the United Nations secret police.

Whose Idea?

The question must surely bang at even the most unsuspecting mind: "What is behind all this?" It would never occur to a Briton - or to a Frenchman or Swede or American, or anyone brought up in the Christian tradition - that national police are not adequate for all civil purposes, so that international police, obedient to an authority perhaps thousands of miles away, should have power to arrest a subject of Her Majesty in Her Majesty's domains, or a French or American citizen or whoever it might be. To whom, then, would such an idea occur? The answer is all too easy. It would occur to the leading members of the only international race, the people who financed the Bolshevik revolution, who turned the United States in the last war into a huge pro-Bolshevist conspiracy, who, as "advisers" to Roosevelt, were responsible for the surrendering of half of Europe to the Tartar hordes, who created U.N.R.R.A.[1] to bolster up the Soviet conquests and at the same time to feed the illegal migration to Palestine, who brought U.N.E.S.C.O.[2] into being as a dual-purpose weapon against Christianity and the pride of race, and whose present preoccupation is to obtain control of all atomic energy to secure for them the rule of the earth. These people, and these people alone, would wish to send their "police" agents with extraterritorial powers to arrest in any country miscreants - such as ourselves - who venture to tell the truth about their financial racket and megalomaniac political designs.

Hidden Power

There is a hidden power, which only to close students of international politics is a revealed power, wielded by a known group of international financial interests, which brought into existence the United Nations and the International Bank as instruments to secure its further advance to world domination.

It has openly declared war on nationhood and racial pride. It approves of every approach, direct or functional, which will render mankind defenceless against its global tyranny. It has used the cold war in the West and the hot wars in Asia to stampede us into N.A.T.O., the European Union and their projected Pacific counterparts. It uses dread

---

[1] The **United Nations Relief and Rehabilitation Administration** was an international relief agency, largely dominated by the United States but theoretically representing 44 nations. UNRRA operated in occupied Germany, primarily in camps for Displaced Persons, especially the 11,000,000 non-Germans who had been moved into Germany during the war, but did not render assistance to ethnic Germans. UNRRA discontinued its operations in Europe on June 30, 1947.

[2] The **United Nations Educational, Scientific and Cultural Organization** is an agency of the United Nations. Its ostensible purpose is to contribute to peace and security by promoting international collaboration through education, science, and culture to further universal respect for justice, the rule of law, and human rights along with fundamental freedom proclaimed in the United Nations Charter. In reality, it is a weapon of the money power and is used to undermine the nation state.

of the H-bomb to try to secure acceptance of its full World Government.

Once our sovereignty is abandoned, and we are completely at its mercy, it will drop its disguise as the foe of Russian aggression and betray us to the Soviet conspiracy as surely as it betrayed us at Yalta through the incredible simpleton Roosevelt, and his incredible adviser, Alger Hiss.[3] Hiss, let it be remembered, was only a fugleman. His protectors were powerful men who constituted - and still constitute - the effective hidden government of the United States.

Socialist Error

Most advocates of World Government are not Communists; many of them are Socialists who abominate Communism. Yet they are blind to the certainty that the integrated world for which they agitate could be no other than a Communist world. In earlier days, Socialists denounced international finance. For thirty years one has heard no such denunciation from them. Is that not on the face of it most strange? When Socialists attack Capitalism, they take care to point to the national industrial capitalists who make goods; they never point to the international loan capitalists who make debts. The reason is that their leaders well understand that the cosmopolitan master-usurers are subversive, waging incessant war against traditional society and ways of life, and therefore appear to be on the side of the Left. Avid careerists, like all other party politicians, they use and are used by these great interests, and never look to the end result. They think that they alone enjoy some special immunity to protect them against the

---

[3] **Alger Hiss** (November 11, 1904 – November 15, 1996) was an American government official who was accused of being a Soviet spy in 1948 and was convicted of perjury in connection with this charge in 1950. Hess maintained his innocence for the rest of his long life, but it appears virtually certain he was indeed a traitor, a liar, and a communist agent.

classic fate of Social Democrats. A fearful error. They will be amongst the first to die.

Carrot and Goad

When the transatlantic origins of the so-called Schuman Plan[4] - in reality the Lilienthal Plan - were pointed out to the M.P. already mentioned, he admitted that support of internationalist schemes might come from Wall Street, but said that as long as they averted the danger of war he did not mind who their sponsors might be. This conjured up the image of a donkey enticed by a carrot called "Peace," and at the same time urged forward with a goad called "War." The carrot and the goad, as it happens, are the specially selected means of snaring and enslaving mankind.

Internationalists of all parties seem to be endowed with some kind of "cut-off" mechanism that prevents their visualising the kind of hell towards which they are leading us.

In developing the theme that power over H-bomb police would make a mockery of so-called constitutional safe-guards, the M.P.'s opponent in the debate mentioned drew a picture of the realisation of the U.N.E.S.C.O. policy of opposition to racial and national discrimination in terms of the invasion of our country, not by a few thousand Jamaicans, but by hundreds of thousands, perhaps millions, of Chinese and Indian immigrants who in "One World" would be as entitled to the absolute use of our island as are the men and women who are native here. If there were objections, as there would be objections, the World Rulers would need to do no more than alert the H-bomb police, against whom there could be no possible resistance or appeal.

---

[4] The **Schuman Declaration** of 9 May 1950 was a governmental proposal by the French Foreign Minister, Robert Schuman, to create a new form of organisation of states in Europe called a "supranational community". It was effectively the forerunner of the European Union.

Undoubtedly in this way we could achieve peace. When the torturers are off duty it is said there is a hushed peace throughout Moscow's Lubyanka Jail.

POLICE STATE PLANS

Plans for the subordination of sovereign nations to a World Government are well advanced. It should be noted how very closely the following proposals and quotations accord, both in method and in phraseology, with the aims that have been consistently pursued for years by international Communism.

At joint conferences of the World Movement for World Federal Government and the World Association of Parliamentarians for World Government, proposals for revision of the United Nations' Charter to introduce World Government by the back door included:

All states shall have a right to membership in the United Nations, provided they accept the terms of the Charter. **Once a state has been admitted into membership, it shall have no right of secession.**

The Charter shall provide for a U.N. Inspectorate to be charged with the supervision of the disarmament plan, and for a U.N. Police to enforce the provisions of the Charter, the laws enacted thereunder, and the decisions of the International Court of Justice and other organs of the U.N.

The Charter shall provide for the creation of lower courts of the U.N., empowered to decide on violations by individuals of the Charter and law enacted thereunder. The International Court of Justice shall have appellate jurisdiction with respect to judgments of such lower courts.

In place of the present General Assembly a World Legislature shall be established. The World Legislature shall consist of two chambers. One Chamber, to be called the Council of States, shall consist of Senators, appointed by the member states. **The other Chamber, to be called the Council of Peoples, shall consist of elected Deputies, the number of Deputies from each member state bearing relation to the population of that state.** All legislation shall be passed by both Chambers.

The World Legislature shall have:

a) Unlimited power of debate and power to make recommendations on any matters within the scope of the Charter or relating to the powers and the functions of any organs provided for in the Charter.

b) Power to raise revenue for U.N. purposes. The maximum percentage of estimated world income to be collected for U.N. purposes must be defined in the Charter, and should be levied proportionately to the national income of each member state.

To ensure that the world law can be enforced by the means of the United Nations against individuals breaking the law, every citizen of a member state shall be a citizen of the U.N. as well as his own country. The Charter and the laws enacted thereunder shall bind each individual citizen of the U.N. The United Nations shall ensure that citizens of non-member states shall act in accordance with the Charter, and the laws enacted thereunder, so far as may be necessary for the maintenance of peace.

The present influence of the Trustee Council in Trust Territories shall be extended to all Colonies and Protectorates.

The privileges and immunities of the officers and agents of the United Nations should be set out in an annexe of the Charter.

The procedure for amending the revised Charter shall ensure that future amendments will not be imposed on non-assenting member states, **unless they embody the views of a substantial majority of the world population.**

A special procedure shall be provided for ratification of the revised Charter to ensure that it would not come into effect **unless supported by a substantial majority of the member states and of the world population.**

"Adequate, world-wide, continued and massive publicity could convey to the peoples of all areas an understanding of the great benefits they might hope for, if disarmament and a World Mutual Development Fund were achieved, and could therefore enlist among the peoples powerful support for such a great proposal and build up strong pressure upon their statesmen to bring this great thing to pass." — *1953 Conference.*

To amend the Statute of the International Court of Justice so as to authorise the establishment of lower United Nations Tribunals to exercise criminal jurisdiction over any individuals accused of offences against international law. — *Interim recommendation,* 1953.

Proposals of the Crusade for World Government include:

Transform the revised United Nations into a world Federal Government responsible to the peoples, and give it authority to:

a) Create a World Development Authority to use the resources of the world for the economic and social progress of all peoples.

b) Control the uses of atomic energy and set up the machinery for international inspection.

c) Replace national armed forces by a world security force with power to arrest and bring before a World Court any individuals who conspire to break the peace of the world.

At the first London World Government Conference, 1951, it was resolved that the Assembly should "Seek to secure that all regional arrangements for federation or defence are so framed that they can be developed or fitted into a system of World Government."

(Since 1943 the U.S.S.R. has concluded many treaties with its satellites. All these treaties are, line for line, almost the same as the North Atlantic Pact Treaty, and all contain an agreement to implement the various clauses **in the spirit of the U.N. Charter.**)

OUT OF THEIR OWN MOUTHS

"We must expect that the international government, once established, will have to widen the sphere of its activities to meet new emergencies. **This almost always happens with federal governments.** The Federal Government of the United States has gradually widened its scope in a manner which would have horrified its founders." — Bertrand Russell, in a broadcast plea for World Government. (*Listener,* 22/7/1954).

"If the U.N. is to be an organisation which can stop war, it must be an effective federal organisation which can take decisions and enforce them. At present the veto prevents it from taking decisions; the veto will have to go. At present the national armed forces can resist the authority of the United Nations; they will have to be disbanded, and at the same time a U.N. Police force must be organised in order to enforce United Nations law." — John Pinder, *U.N. Reform*. Federal Union.

"The postulation of agreement or consent as a requisite must always be regarded with a wary eye... The idea of consent is closely identified with plebiscites and nationalism, the powerful dogma of self-determination." — Dr. G.C. Mangone, *The Idea and Practice of World Government*.

"Assuming that one power dissented with the proposals, what would be the legal position? The Charter of the United Nations would not be changed, but do you believe that the majority would consent to this? I feel convinced that they would do what the Swiss did in 1848 when the overwhelming majority in favour of federation imposed their will on the minority." — Dr. Max Habicht, Switzerland, at 4th World Parl. Conf. on World Govt., London, 1954.

"If we cannot attain to universalism and create union by common consent and democratic methods as a result of rational thinking - then rather than retard the process let us precipitate unification by conquest." — Mr. Emery Reeves.

"There can be no naive assumption that the heavens will be moved and the kingdom of darkness rolled away without the use of force... Without a determination to add combat soldiers to the economic attacks on poverty and the intellectual attacks upon intolerant provincialism, any primary organisation looking toward one democratic world will fail." — Dr. Gerard C. Mangone, *The Idea and Practice of Word Government*.

"It would seem worth considering whether the conference should be held in Moscow. We cannot expect miracles, and I think it would be wise policy to propose such changes as are reasonably acceptable to the Russians." — Dr. A. Vondeling, M.P. Netherlands, at 4th World Parl. Conf. on World Govt. London, 1954.

"How much of national sovereignty must be surrendered? It is that aspect that frightens most of those who view our movement with distrust... We would do well to emphasise that this is **initially** all we ask - the warring and contesting nations to surrender the right to decide their own disputes and the right to vindicate their decision by force of arms to some higher international institution." — J.E.S. Simon, M.P. At 4th World Parl. Conf. on World Government, London, 1954.

"The necessity of Charter Revision must seem obvious to the people, who are now forced to realise that the concept of sovereignty is not only outdated but nonsense, and that federalism is the only alternative to it." — Lord Beveridge, at Conf. of Organisations on Revision of the U.N. Charter. 26/2/1955.

"We cannot please ourselves by performing only minor amputations on the tree of national sovereignty. If national sovereignty is not dealt with **in toto**, but only relatively, it will recuperate at a propitious moment, assume its former robust character and wreak a new vengeance on mankind. Nothing can prostrate national sovereignty so much as the loss of control over physical force by the nation state." — Mr. Nicholas Doman, *The Coming Age of World Control*.

"All these promises (in the United Nations Charter) have been broken. The explanation is simple. The Charter accepted the principle of national sovereignty." — John Pinder, *U.N. Reform*. Federal Union.

"I would ask whether the United Nations can be an effective organ if national sovereignty is not limited. The nations must sacrifice a part of their sovereignty if the United Nations is to be a real and effective organ." — Mr. Vyshinsky.

"The civil service and police would be **very carefully selected** and trained, to ensure that they were loyal **exclusively** to the United Nations... the United Nations would protect them from victimisation from their own state for actions performed in the service of the United Nations." — John Pinder. *U.N. Reform*. Fed. Union.

"The day is not far off when representatives of all the nations will assemble **in a single sovereign parliament** just as we have gathered here - when a single flag shall fly over all the lands and seas of the earth, and men shall see no soldiers but the soldiers of mankind." — Shahoodul Huque, M.P. Pakistan, at 4th World Parl. Conf. on World Govt. London, 1954.

"There cannot be a world-state without the prerequisite of a world nation as a basis... The Islamic ideals of brotherhood and the equality of man... unmistakably indicate that the Islamic conception is not only in perfect accord with the idea, but also offers a practicable scheme for the ultimate establishment of a World State." — Hon. Tamizuddin Khan, Pakistan. March, 1950.

"It is conceivable that the principles prevailing in the supernational political structure will not be acceptable to some or all of the organised religions. Representatives of these religions might challenge the political authority and scheme for its removal... If religion linked its cause with nationalism and the nation-state, it might well share their fate... In the case of the religious challenge, the political authority might attempt to restrict or ban the activities of the Church." — Mr. Nicholas Doman, *The Coming Age of World Control*.

"Perhaps this conference might be inclined to draw up a draft for a World Population Fund, half at least of the resources of which, in my opinion, should be devoted to a most important single piece of research - the provision of a simple foolproof and cheap contraceptive." — Professor Julian Huxley, at 4th World Parl. Conf. on World Govt., London, 1954.

JOIN THE LEAGUE OF EMPIRE LOYALISTS

Chairman: D. S. Fraser Harris

Organising Secretary:
Miss M. C. Greene, M.A.

Hon. Treasurer:
W. A. Brooks

EXECUTIVE COMMITTEE

Major G. B. J. Athoe, A.Inst.N.A., M.Inst.R.A.
Mrs. L. Belam
A. K. Chesterton
Mrs. M. Clarkson
F. Clifford
A. G. Evans
R. D. Jeune

Colin Jordan, M.A.
Aidan Mackey
Mrs. Joyce Mew
George Pile
Captain A. Rogers, O.B.E.
Lt. Col. J. Creagh Scott, D.S.O., O.B.
T. S. Stewart
L. A. Stokes, A.P.C.A.
George Tillett.

NATIONAL COUNCIL:

The Earl of Buchan
Field-Marshal Lord Ironside, G.C.B., C.M.G., D.S.O.
Lt. Col. T. B. Butt (late of Kenya)
Mrs. I. Byng-Morris
W. K. A. J. Chambers-Hunter
Cllr. Guy Collis
Elizabeth Lady Freeman, M.B.E.
Cllr. Joseph Holden, F.N.I.C.S.
Group Captain R. D. Leather
S. Mackay
Peter Marriott
Air Commodore G. S. Oddie, D.F.C., A.F.C.
Sir Richmond Palmer, K.C.M.G., C.B.E.
Miss Alice Raven
Derek Tozer, M.A.
W/Cdr. L. Young

AUSTRALIA
M. A. Blake
Eric D. Butler
A. W. Noakes

CANADA
Lt. Commander T. W. Bridges, R.N.R. (Retd.)
A. T. Klassen
Mrs. C. Nesbit

CEYLON
J. M. E. Waring

NEW ZEALAND
Sir Ernest H. Andrews, K.B., C.B.E.
T. Armstrong
J. Hartley
F. W. Stevens

SOUTH AFRICA
Miss V. Couchman
Air Commodore C. H. Elliott-Smith, A.F.C.

S. RHODESIA
C. Geneve
C. M. Heanley, M.B.
Mrs. I. B. Wemyss

KENYA
Mrs. C. Belfrage
Cmdr. G. J. Llewellyn, R.N.
G. Ogilvie, F.R.I.B.A.
D. P. Proctor
Major B. P. Roberts

SINGAPORE
N. W. H. Gray

and fight for
BRITISH INDEPENDENCE

Particulars from :
11, PALACE CHAMBERS, BRIDGE STREET, WESTMINSTER, S.W.1
Telephone : TRAfalgar 3881

This is the back cover of the original L.E.L. edition of *The Menace of World Government* and it gives an excellent indication of the League's empire wide membership in the mid 1950's.

BRITAIN'S GRAVEYARD

Dangers of the Common Market

By A.K. Chesterton

ROAD TO RUIN

The Prime Minister[5] has been swift off the mark to take such steps as are needed to bring about the total disintegration of the British Empire. Our destiny, he told a B.B.C. audience recently, is to tie Europe and the British Commonwealth to be a force comparable with the U.S.A. and Russia.

"Britain is not alone," he said. "Think of the Commonwealth and all that it means. Think also of the peoples of Europe. With these countries, with France perhaps particularly, we already have close ties. I firmly believe that it is our destiny to work more and more closely with them. The total of the strength and wealth of all these communities, Commonwealth and Europe, is no less than that of the two giant powers."

Astute Timing

Although the policy Mr. Macmillan announced is not new - did not Lenin urge the creation of the United States of Europe? - he has been astute in forcing the issue to the forefront at the present time.

---

[5] **Harold Macmillan** (10 February 1894 – 29 December 1986) was a British Conservative politician and statesman who served as the Prime Minister from 10 January 1957 to 18 October 1963.

The British people are basically anti-communist. As a result of recent events in Suez most of them have had their eyes opened to the game played by the United States and are also anti-American. What better way to cash in on upon this state of mind than for the British Government to promise to unite with Europe to create a third force which would be able to hold its own against either the United States of America or the Soviet Union!

That the process sooner or later must involve the smashing of our sovereign independence - an objective which Macmillan in his more candid moments has openly declared to be his aim - was not mentioned in his broadcast.

It is not only that the United States of Europe, towards which the creation of a European common market will be a big step forward, is an avowedly Communist concept: even more sinister is the fact that the financial forces in control of American policy have been ceaselessly plotting since before the war to force the European nations to abandon their sovereignty and federate. Successive Supreme Allied Commanders of the North Atlantic Treaty Organisation and successive administrators of American aid have all faithfully followed the policy laid down by their masters.

Is it seriously supposed that the United States would use its immense power to bring about a European federation if the masters of American policy believed for one moment that in so doing they would not build up a rival of "equal strength and wealth"? Of course not.

"American" Requirement

We have seen with what ease the Transatlantic wire-pullers were able to use economic pressure to ensure the instant and most humiliating withdrawal of the Franco-British troops from the Middle-East. We have seen how the subsequent fuel crisis obliged our Government to go cap-in-hand to the international usurers for another huge loan, thereby increasing still further their power of economic leverage.

It is therefore certain that no major act of policy in the United Kingdom at the present time is being carried out in the teeth of "American" hostility. More than that, it is certain that every major act of British policy in the field of foreign affairs is an "American" requirement. What the Prime Minister - with the full approval of the Socialist leaders - represents as a challenge to the might of the United States is in fact itself a major act of United States policy. **Unless the British people can be made to understand this fact now they will be utterly and irretrievably ruined.**

CONSERVATIVE PLEDGE!

"The principle of granting Preference, which has been the lifeline of our Commonwealth, and in particular of our Colonies, must be preserved" - Industrial Charter, 1947.

GRAND OBJECTIVE

Great Britain's economy and the economies of the other Commonwealth countries are largely complementary, yet Government policy is not to strengthen these economic ties but to weaken them, by creating a free trade area with foreign countries whose economics compete with our own.

Mr. Macmillan, however, is not the man to be frightened of competition, "It is surely wrong," he told the House of Commons, "to talk about competition as if it has some sinister ring." "Ring" is the *mot juste*! The grand objective of financial and industrial competition has long been elimination of the other competitors, which is precisely the end that the promoters of the common market (we mean the real promoters, not the Government stooges) are determined to achieve.

Proponent of Centralisation

Mr. Macmillan cannot have forgotten the idealistic part he played in the 'thirties as a member of *Political and Economic Planning*, because it is to his activities at that time that he may well owe his present position. "Competition" then had a sufficiently "sinister ring" to make Harold Macmillan a leading proponent of the doctrine of centralised economic control - in other words, of monopoly disporting itself in the guise of "rationalisation".

What stands in the way of the extension of that doctrine to Europe and the world is the national sovereignty which enables Governments with sufficient guts to thwart the will of the would-be central controllers - **the sovereignty which the British Government is now preparing to abandon.**

Abandon it they will, because Britain's participation in the European free trade area must entail her progressively closer association with, and final submergence in, the actual common market. She will thus be subjected to the requirement that, after the transitional stage, any worker from any of the nations participating in the common market may take employment or set up business in any of the countries beside his own. That implies, if not a common citizenship, beyond doubt the elimination of the rights of nations to preserve a homogeneous population.

Frenchmen will have as much right to Germany as Germans will have to Holland or as Italians will have to Belgium. This is not even internationalism by stealth, although the general agreement to "play it down" gives that impression. It is the most blatant internationalist enactment so far attempted.

Common Welfare State

Workers are also to be protected against the loss of pension rights and other social security benefits when they work in other countries. It may be thought that this will involve no more than a series of book-keeping entries and contra-accounts, but in fact what is clearly projected is a Common Welfare State.

Even more onerous is the requirement that within four years the treaty nations will be obliged to recognise each other's teaching diplomas, medical degrees and other specialised qualifications. Only a very vague person could suppose that standards will thereby be improved: they can only be lowered.

DO THEY MEAN WHAT THEY SAY?

"The Conservative Party has never supported any decision taken at Geneva, Havana or elsewhere, inimical to the general system of Imperial Preference, and we shall take all steps in our power to ensure that in the future our liberty in this direction is not impaired" - *Imperial Policy*, 1949.

"We shall retain Imperial Preference and uphold the right to grant and receive such preferences as are mutually agreed with Empire countries. The Empire producer will have a place in the home market second only to the home producer." - *Britain Strong and Free*, 1951.

TOWARDS MONOPOLY

Perhaps the Prime Minister did not read the special article in the *Daily Telegraph* by Mr. John Applebey, explaining how and why we should associate ourselves with the proposed European common market. The article reveals - perhaps without knowing it - the true significance of that project. If *Daily Telegraph* readers are not aware of the revelation, or if, being aware of it, they are not horrified at what it portends, then not only they but the nation and the whole Western world are in a desperate intellectual plight.

"It is in the minds of the sponsors of the market," declares Mr. Applebey, "that there would be a merging of productive facilities until there might be, for example, only two motor manufacturers for all six countries." Is it conceivable that men and women of education, as *Daily Telegraph* readers are presumed to be, can accept a proposition like this with the equanimity with which it is presented to them?

"Double-Speak"

Before taking a closer look at the passage quoted, let us collate with it the passage which follows: "To this end it is part of the scheme that the countries concerned should set up a European Commission to run the market. It would have powers of trust-busting...."

Incredible? Yes, that is the only word to describe it. Mr. Applebey's naiveté is the measure of his honesty. Only an honest man would dare to place these two passages in juxtaposition. "Double-think" and "double-speak", which we tend to regard as the contrivances of wicked people, have become the normal processes of the innocent - a fact that certainly does not lessen their peril. When a newspaper of the standing enjoyed by the *Telegraph* allows the concept of "a merging of productive facilities" to be written down as though it were the complement, and not the antithesis, of "truth-busting", then human speech has been so far debased that we begin to think with some relish of the Shakespearean line: "The rest is silence."

Incidentally, there are no more stringent anti-trust laws than in the United States, which is the home of gigantic trusts. These laws, where they are not completely inoperative, seem to serve the exclusive purpose of enabling the dominant money monopoly to hit would-be competitors on the head. Hence the suggestion that similar powers be invested in the European Commission which is to run the common market.

To return to Mr. Applebey's first passage. Why does he suggest that the "merging of productive facilities" would continue until there might be - to give his own example - "only two motor manufacturers for all six countries"? What would prevent the number being reduced to one? The crafty "sponsors", whom Applebey seems so much to admire, no doubt prefer for the sake of appearances to give the lie to any ungenerous critic who might otherwise accuse them of establishing a monopoly.

Commissioners - or Commissars?

As long as there are two motor manufacturers, over no matter how large an area, it will always be possible to maintain the pretence of competition. What would prevent a secret understanding between the two vast firms? Indeed, is it not certain that they would be twin expressions of one and the same economic power? If John Applebey is correctly informed, as no doubt he is, the European common market is to be nothing other than a slightly disguised European Communist State. Whether those who will run the various industrial trusts are called Commissioners or Commissars would not seem to matter very much. Yet Applebey and the editor who publicises his views have so little awareness of politico-economic realities that *Daily Telegraph* readers are asked to regard the embryonic monstrosity with approval, being assured that it "may become one of the most exciting and important post-war economic developments".

Such simplicity of mind and soul in supposedly responsible publicists is staggering. We wonder whether the "little man", already battling for his life in every part of Europe, is equally excited at the prospect of his absorption by the giant monopolies now being incubated.

It is the purpose of the common market not to study the feelings of the "little man" but to eradicate him. Mr. Applebey in effect tells us that this is the actual policy of the sponsors of the scheme. The European Commission which runs the market will have power of absolute decision over the whole field of the European economy. If the small firms protest, their directors will not necessarily be sent to Siberian labour camps - though it may come to that - for the simple reason that the Commissioners will have the power overnight to cut off their labour force and supplies of raw materials. Nor will the labourers have a say in the matter. Mr. Applebey, without any visible shudder, tells us that the Commission will have authority to "retrain and resettle displaced workers".

Should Britain adhere to the set up, and should, let us say, the Morris company be wound up by order of the monopolists, the Commissioners could decide to retrain its skilled engineers as deep-sea fishermen and send them from Oxford to live in Iceland or the Baltic. Should this be to take an extreme view of the possibilities inherent in the European market scheme, who can doubt that the various trade union movements would be required to federate, with no right for workers to contract out? That might amount to much the same thing.

Authority to Meddle

Nor, if we are to believe Mr. Applebey, will the European Commission be content to dominate the economic scene. It will have "the authority to harmonise the individual countries' social policies". That means nothing unless it means the authority to meddle in the political affairs of member nations and to dictate how the tax-payers' money is to be allocated in the provision of welfare services.

Such authority would provide the foundation for an ultimate authority over every aspect of Europe's political life, and this general authority could only function as a dictatorship. It would rule Europeans as remorselessly as the Kremlin rules the lives of the Soviet masses. There would be nothing to prevent the two dictatorships coalescing, and that, we are convinced, would be not only the natural development of the common market, but - all unknown to Mr. Applebey and his editor - the fulfilment of the evil design already planned.

If the Prime Minister did not read the article, he must surely have recognised his scheme of rationalism in the 'thirties reappearing in a wider context. It is scarcely conceivable, of course, that he can be ignorant of these larger ambitions now entertained for ideas once so precious to him, but he did not see fit to take Parliament into his confidence about them.

Nor can Mr. Macmillan have forgotten that "P.E.P"[6], which concerned itself with "Capitalist" planning, worked in close co-operation with the Fabian Society, which concerned itself with "Socialist" planning. Simpletons may suppose that the two sets of planners are as armies embattled against each other: if they do, the reason is that the simpletons have no clue about the organisation of power in the modern world.

---

[6] **Political and Economic Planning (PEP)** was a British policy think tank, formed in 1931 It was influential in the formation of the National Health Service, World War II and post-war planning, and the development of the African colonies. In 1978 PEP merged with the Centre for the Study of Social Policy, and became the Policy Studies Institute.

More Controls!

Harold Macmillan, at all events, cannot have been surprised at the welcome given to the common market proposal by the Opposition, or have been greatly disconcerted to hear Mr. Harold Wilson[7] say:

"We therefore regard this plan, if appropriate arrangements can be made in the negotiations so that we can enter it, not as a generalisation of a free economy, but as a change of policy which will require very fundamental changes of internal policy in this country. This is our chance, our one chance to increase investment, and in our view this will mean more controls, more positive Socialist planning measures, more positive use of public ownership, not only to increase the total volume of investment in this country, but also to direct that investment more purposively into the industries we most need to expand."

No wonder the Prime Minister told the Commons that the course to be pursued was not one upon which the Government felt it could launch "as a purely party matter" and that "it would not be right to start on this course unless there was a reasonable assurance that all parties in the State and all sections of industry were, by and large, prepared to give a general support to it. That is why we have sought advice from industry and from the trade unions, and now come to Parliament".

---

[7] **Harold Wilson** (11 March 1916 – 24 May 1995) was a British Labour Party politician who served as the Prime Minister from 1964 to 1970 and 1974 to 1976. He won four general elections.

TOEING LENIN'S LINE

The European market has to be presented as all things to all men, but what it really amounts to is a scheme whereby planners of the so-called Right may co-operate with planners of the so-called Left (as in the 'thirties) in clearing a path for European - and World - Communism. Macmillan and Wilson, whether they know it or not, are rivals for the Kerensky role. And of the two Macmillan is "the elder and more terrible".

What is more, underlying the economic approach is the political approach towards Communism which takes the form - one form among many - of a drive for European federation. Considering the significance of the federalism implicit, though as yet only adumbrated, in the common market proposal, it would have been to the Prime Minister's credit had he done more than merely hint at the political development which he believes will follow its acceptance. His son, making his maiden speech, was intellectually more honest. He hoped that the scheme would lead to "a truly united Europe". When national sovereignty has been destroyed, and when Mr. Wilson is not only in possession of "more controls, more positive Socialist planning measures, more positive use of public ownership" but possesses them on a federal scale, then who in his senses can suppose that we shall be anything other than slaves in the European Union of Soviet Socialist Republics?

Destruction of Sovereignty

Even those who would regard this as an extreme view cannot fail to see that both the Macmillan record in support of "rationalisation" and the Socialist hopes of increased scope for public ownership and control, together with what has become known of the intentions of the promoters, combine to make of the European common market idea a device whereby ever fewer men will regulate down to the last detail the livelihood of vast populations, with ever decreasing possibilities for individuals to "contract out".

The British right to "contract out" is being weakened, already to the point of destruction, by the abrogation of British sovereignty. Sovereignty can only be upheld by an island nation such as our own by the maintenance of power overseas - economic power as well as military power.

Damnable Betrayal

Aware that half our trade is with the other Commonwealth and Empire countries, Mr Macmillan pleaded on behalf of his European free trade area proposals that by the exclusion of agricultural products, they would leave ninety per cent of the trade protected by Imperial Preference unaffected. In as far as preferential rates are based on pre-war values, and in as far as our adherence to Gatt[8] renders us powerless to upgrade or extend them, the official admission that the Commonwealth system will be further weakened, by the removal of preferential tariff protection from ten per cent of the goods now covered by it, adds yet another damnable betrayal to the many betrayals by which the British peoples are being progressively robbed of their heritage.

Lenin once laid down that the best means of subverting the Western nations was to attack them at the periphery - that is, to break up their indispensable bulwark of overseas power, possessions and spheres of influence. British Governments in this respect have long been following the Leninist line, and the present Prime Minister,

---

[8] The **General Agreement on Tariffs and Trade (GATT)** was a multilateral agreement regulating international trade. Its purpose was the "substantial reduction of tariffs and other trade barriers and the elimination of preferences, on a reciprocal and mutually advantageous basis."

enthusiastically supported by the Socialist Opposition, is now preparing for it a great and perhaps decisive victory.

REALLY?

"Her Majesty's Government attaches great importance to Imperial Preference, not only as a symbol of the desires of the countries of the Commonwealth to stand together and to trade with each other, but also as a practical means of increasing their trade and their prosperity." - Mr. Peter Thorneycroft, House of Commons, 1952.

WARNING TO WORKERS

Although he supports the common market, Mr. C.J. Geddes[9], the former chairman of the T.U.C. General Council, has admitted that acceptance of the conception by the British trade union movement would mean that "the British worker would have to make temporary sacrifices, even to the extent, if necessary, of accepting a lower standard of living to raise the standard of living of the workers in the more backward countries in Europe."

This calls for two comments. Firstly, the sacrifices would not be temporary. Secondly, it is to betray stark mental confusion to suppose that a higher standard of living can be secured by distributing, as it were, a lower standard of living.

---

[9] **Charles John Geddes** (1 March 1897 – 2 May 1983) was a British trade unionist.

In any case, why should British workers be expected to impoverish themselves to increase the pay-packets of Greeks? Why should they condemn themselves and their families to unemployment to find work for Italians?

Is It Selfish?

Mr. Geddes's chief answer seems to be altruism: "It is a conception against which it is difficult to find valid arguments provided that one is prepared to consider the problem from a European trade union point of view rather than a somewhat more selfish national point of view."

Is it selfish for a British worker to give preference to feeding his own child? Is it selfish for him to wish his family to enjoy the advantages which have accrued to Britain through the skill, industry and enterprise of her sons and daughters at home and over the seas?

By all means let us do what we can to help peoples less fortunate than we are, but not at the expense of those who have the right to look to us for the substance of life and for some of its amenities.

Yet every idealist, every superficialist, every careerist, every publicity-seeking hound in the United Kingdom seems to be clamouring for Great Britain to become the dupe of this concealed Communist plot. There is a belief among these British sheep that the more they can be herded with other sheep the fatter and richer and more secure they will become.

It is true that Great Britain must have large overseas markets. What the Government shows no desire to explain is why we do not rebuild, in terms of modem values, our own Imperial economic system which stood us in good stead during the 'thirties and which - had there been in this country the will - could have been enormously extended after the last war.

Tendentious Statement

The Government's sole concern is to entice us away from any such idea by depicting in extravagantly luscious phrases the attractions of the idea which must ultimately annihilate it. Thus another Conservative publication, entitled *Europe Free Trade*, contains this shockingly tendentious statement:

"Free entry to a market of 240-300 million is a morsel which should make any business man's mouth (not to speak of the mouths of his employees) water in anticipation of the rich pickings...."

It were kinder, perhaps, not to comment on the sort of language which the Conservative Central Office believes to be inspiring, but one is nevertheless constrained to ask (1) What of the free entry into Britain of goods produced by cheap Continental labour? and (2) Are the mouths of the business man's employees watering at the thought of the unemployment doles which will be the inevitable result?

Expansion of the system of Imperial Preference[10] would involve none of the hardship and misery of the European common market scheme. Why, then, do we not undertake it?

To strive to bring about the economic integration of Europe could only mean a still further dissipation of the British heritage, leading to eventual chaos not only in Europe but throughout the world.

---

[10] **Imperial Preference** was a proposed system of reciprocally-enacted tariffs or free trade agreements between the dominions and colonies of the British Empire. The United States was determined to maintain its tariff protections and access to markets, and was vociferously opposed to any such preferences enjoyed by other countries. Great Britain was therefore forced into the European federation, and the United States had eliminated a rival on the world stage.

Mr. MACMILLAN ON FREE TRADE

"The logic of this theory is that when other countries are able to produce and sell any commodity at a lower price than we can produce it ourselves, we should transfer our labour and capital resources to the production of something else. Thus, with the stroke of a pen, the Free Trade economist will dismiss the whole human tragedy which lies between. The industry will not close down without a struggle. To struggle means that it will cut its cost; in the last analysis this involves the cutting of wages. It is true that the cost of the imported commodities will fall for the community generally, but the losses will be concentrated upon the workers still engaged in the doomed industry. The cost of living will not fall for them as rapidly as their incomes are reduced." - *The Middle Way*, 1938.

INDUSTRIALISTS' VIEW

The Federation of British Industries did not as a body oppose the Government's proposals to enter into negotiations with a view to joining the free trade area, but complained in a letter to the President of the Board of Trade that there had been "widespread dissatisfaction with the lack of time to consider these complex issues." The latter stated: Those industries which are strongly opposed to negotiations put forward the following principle reasons for their view:

(1) They fear the flooding of their home markets with no compensating advantages in freer entry to the European markets;

(2) They consider that other European countries enjoy natural advantages which cannot be overtaken by improvements in efficiency. This is particularly true where another country has domestic supplies of raw materials not available in the United Kingdom, e.g. wood pulp;

(3) They are deeply sceptical of the possibility in practice of working out watertight safeguards which would enable competition to be conducted on level terms.

IF GREAT BRITAIN

is associated with the

EUROPEAN COMMON MARKET

in a

FREE TRADE AREA

it will mean that:

(1) European goods produced by cheap foreign labour will flood the country;

(2) Hundreds of British firms will be forced into bankruptcy;

(3) Thousands, and perhaps millions, of British workers will lose their jobs;

(4) Britain's living standards will tumble to Continental levels;

(5) Commonwealth manufactured goods will be driven out of the British market by foreign manufactured goods;

(6) Eventually, in the European Federation - of which the common market is the foundation stone - foreigners will have as much right to Britain as have the British people themselves.

About A.K. Chesterton

Arthur Kenneth Chesterton was born at the Luipaards Vlei gold mine, Krugersdorp, South Africa where his father was an official in 1899.

In 1915 unhappy at school in England A.K. returned to South Africa. There and without the knowledge of his parents, and having exaggerated his age by four years, he enlisted in the 5th South African Infantry.

Before his 17th birthday he had been in the thick of three battles in German East Africa. Later in the war he transferred as a commissioned officer to the Royal Fusiliers and served for the rest of the war on the Western Front being awarded the Military Cross in 1918 for conspicuous gallantry.

Between the wars A.K. first prospected for diamonds before becoming a journalist first in South Africa and then England. Alarmed at the economic chaos threatening Britain, he joined Sir Oswald Mosley in the B.U.F and became prominent in the movement. In 1938, he quarrelled with Mosley's policies and left the movement.

When the Second World War started he rejoined the army, volunteered for tropical service and went through all the hardships of the great push up from Kenya across the wilds of Jubaland through the desert of the Ogaden and into the remotest parts of Somalia. He was afterwards sent down the coast to join the Somaliland Camel Corps and intervene in the inter-tribal warfare among the Somalis.

In 1943 his health broke down and he was invalided out of the army with malaria and colitis, returning to journalism. In 1944, he became deputy editor and chief leader writer of *Truth*.

In the early 1950s A.K. established *Candour* and founded the League of Empire Loyalists which for some years made many colourful headlines in the press worldwide. He later took that organisation into The National Front, and served as its Chairman for a time.

A.K. Chesterton died in 1973.

A.K. Chesterton

About The A.K. Chesterton Trust

The A.K. Chesterton Trust was formed by Colin Todd and the late Miss. Rosine de Bounevialle in January 1996 to succeed and continue the work of the now defunct Candour Publishing Co.

The objects of the Trust are stated as follows:

"To promote and expound the principles of A.K. Chesterton which are defined as being to demonstrate the power of, and to combat the power of International Finance, and to promote the National Sovereignty of the British World."

Our aims include:

- *Maintaining and expanding the range of material relevant to A.K. Chesterton and his associates throughout his life.*

- *To preserve and keep in-print important works on British Nationalism in order to educate the current generation of our people.*

- *The maintenance and recovery of the sovereign independence of the British Peoples throughout the world.*

- *The strengthening of the spiritual and material bonds between the British Peoples throughout the world.*

- *The resurgence at home and abroad of the British spirit.*

We will raise funds by way of merchandising and donations.

We ask that our friends make provision for *The A.K. Chesterton Trust* in their will.

The A.K. Chesterton Trust has a **duty** to keep *Candour* in the ring and punching.

CANDOUR: To defend national sovereignty against the menace of international finance.

CANDOUR: To serve as a link between Britons all over the world in protest against the surrender of their world heritage.

Subscribe to Candour

CANDOUR SUBSCRIPTION RATES FOR 10 ISSUES.

U.K. £30.00
Europe 50 Euros.
Rest of the World £45.00.
USA $60.00.

All Airmail. Cheques and Postal Orders, £'s Sterling only, made payable to *The A.K. Chesterton Trust*. (Others, please send cash by **secure post**, $ bills or Euro notes.)

Payment by Paypal is available. Please see our website **www.candour.org.uk** for more information.

Candour Back Issues

Back issues are available. 1953 to the present.

Please request our back issue catalogue by sending your name and address with two 1st class stamps to:

The A.K. Chesterton Trust, BM Candour, London, WC1N 3XX, UK

Alternatively, see our website at **www.candour.org.uk** where you can order a growing selection on-line.

British Peoples League

Britons Unite Worldwide

Box 691, Minden, Ontario. K0M 2K0, Canada.

www.britishpeoplesleague.com

Broadsword

The official supporting publication of the British Movement

For a sample copy of their 24-page Journal send £2.00 payable to *Broadsword* at:

PO Box 6, Heckmondwicke, WF16 0XF, England

Heritage and Destiny

Nationalist News & Views

For a sample copy of Heritage & Destiny, please send £5.00 payable to the same at:
40 Birkett Drive, Preston, PR2 6HE, England

The London Forum

The London Forum hosts regular meetings in Central London on a Pan-Nationalist theme with a wide range of speakers from across Europe and the World.

For more information please email: jezenglish@yahoo.co.uk

The A.K. Chesterton Trust Reprint Series

1. Creed of a Fascist Revolutionary & Why I Left Mosley - A.K. Chesterton.

2. The Menace of World Government & Britain's Graveyard - A.K. Chesterton.

3. What You Should Know About The United Nations - The League of Empire Loyalists.

4. The Menace of the Money-Power - A.K. Chesterton.

5. The Case for Economic Nationalism - John Tyndall.

6. Sound the Alarm! - A.K. Chesterton.

7. Six Principles of British Nationalism - John Tyndall.

8. B.B.C. - A National Menace - A.K. Chesterton.

9. Stand by the Empire - A.K. Chesterton.

10. Tomorrow. A Plan for the British Future - A.K. Chesterton.

11. The British Constitution and the Corruption of Parliament - Ben Greene.

Other Titles from *The A.K. Chesterton Trust*

Leopard Valley - A.K. Chesterton.

Juma The Great - A.K. Chesterton.

The New Unhappy Lords - A.K. Chesterton.

Facing The Abyss - A.K. Chesterton.

The History of the League of Empire Loyalists - McNeile & Black

All the above titles are available from The A.K. Chesterton Trust, BM Candour, London, WC1N 3XX, UK

www.candour.org.uk

22227941R00028

Printed in Great Britain
by Amazon